Contents

Welcome — A great place to live

1 Look and write.

1 I'm Leo. I live in a ___village___ (ivgalel) in a house next to the _____ (rbdgei). Today I'm at the _____ (tCiy lHla).

2 Hi! I'm Bella. I live in a _____ (tfla) near the _____ (tciy ncerte).

3 Hello! I'm Sam. I live in a tall _____ (bduingil) on a big _____ (setert).

4 Hi! I'm Nadia. I live on a _____ (afmr) near some _____ (hlsli) and _____ (dfleis).

2 Read and write. Then write for you.

show ~~talk~~ help learn

1 ___What does___ Leo like doing in the village?
___He likes talking___ to people.

2 _____ Sam like doing in the city?
_____ about different cultures.

3 _____ Bella _____ doing in the city?
_____ animals.

4 _____ Nadia _____ on the farm?
_____ people the countryside.

5 I like _____.

6 I _____.

3 (0.09) Listen and write the dates. Then number.

___1940___ [2] _____ ☐ _____ ☐ _____ ☐ _____ ☐ _____ ☐

Extra time? Think of three dates. Tell a partner to write them.

4 Listen and complete for Linda. Then complete for you and write.

On a school day...	Linda	You
What time do you wake up?	6:50	
What time do you have lunch?		
What time to you go to bed?		

1 Linda _wakes up at ten to seven._   **4** I wake up at _____.

2 She _____.   **5** I _____.

3 She _____.   **6** I _____.

5 Find and circle nine countries. Then do the Countries Quiz.

O	M	E	X	I	C	O	B	N	L
F	W	G	R	E	Y	A	P	N	C
S	P	A	I	N	B	M	B	M	K
U	O	F	E	X	S	U	S	A	F
K	A	R	G	E	N	T	I	N	A
Z	X	I	T	A	L	Y	Y	L	J
U	J	N	U	K	P	J	K	D	I
C	H	I	N	A	V	X	S	B	P
G	T	U	R	K	E	Y	J	K	G
W	T	I	P	O	L	A	N	D	T

1 Where can you find the city, Pontevedra? ___Spain___

2 Where is there a Tree Planting Day every year? _____

3 Where can you see plants on bridges and buildings? _____, _____, _____

4 Where do children help people with their shopping? _____

5 Where do people play board games in the park? _____

6 Where do people celebrate the Children's Festival? _____

7 Where do people make plates and bowls from plants? _____

I can shine!

6 Write about you.

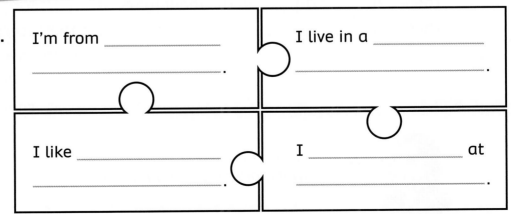

I'm from _____.

I live in a _____.

I like _____.

I _____ at _____.

Exploring wildlife

Let's review!

Write three animals that live in the ocean.

_____ _____ _____

1 Look and write *a*, *e*, *i*, *o* or *u*.

| 1 | 2 | 3 | 4 | 5 |

d _e_ _e_ r   p__l__r b____r   ch____t__h   ____gl____   t__rt____s__

| 6 | 7 | 8 | 9 | 10 |

k___ng__r____   b____tl__   c__m__l   cr__c__d__l__   w__lf

2 Look at Activity 1 and write.

1 There's a _____wolf_____ in the mountains.

2 There's a _____ in the desert.

3 _____ in the river.

4 _____ sky.

5 _____ snow.

Tell me!

Which animals are on grass? _____

_____

Extra time? Order the animals from big to small. Compare with a partner.

1 Listen and tick (✓). Then match to make sentences.

 a    b    c    d

1   A polar bear is bigger   a   in the snow.

2   A polar bear lives   b   white.

3   A polar bear   c   a polar bear.

4   A polar bear is   d   is bigger than a wolf.

5   A wolf is smaller than   e   than a tortoise.

2 Look, choose and write.

1   A tortoise _is slower than a cheetah._   (slow / fast)

2   A rabbit _____. (tall / short)

3   A deer _____. (cute / scary)

4   A polar bear _____. (big / small)

5   A kangaroo _____. (slow / fast)

I can shine!

3 Choose your favourite animal. Write a riddle for a partner.

It's _____.

It lives _____.

It's _____ than a _____.

It's _____.

 Extra time? Make flashcards of new words.

5

1 **Read and write G (girl), W (wolf) or GR (grandmother). Then number.**

☐ *I can go to the forest.* _____

1 *We need wood for the fire.* GR

☐ *Take some wood, but don't cut down our trees.* _____

☐ *Stop! I want to talk to you.* _____

☐ *You're safe!* _____

☐ *We should plant more trees.* _____

Let's imagine!
Tell me about the story!
The story setting is
_____.
My favourite character is
_____.

2 **Read and write.**

1 The girl is ____young.____ (nuogy)

2 The monkeys are _____ in the tree. (fsea)

3 The deer is _____. (lfridyne)

4 Trees are _____. (tpimnaort)

5 The wolf isn't _____. (gdnruoaes)

6 The girl is _____. (iegitltneln)

I can shine!

3 **How can you help wildlife? Write.**

I can _____.

I can _____.

I can _____.

Extra time? Why are trees important? Write three reasons.

1 **Order and write.**

1 I think cheetahs __are more beautiful than kangaroos.__
kangaroos / more / are / than / beautiful

2 I think hockey _____ .
dangerous / is / more / snowboarding / than

3 I think people _____ .
than / animals / intelligent / are / more

4 _____
think / Science / English / I / interesting / than / more / is

5 _____
I / cats / think / cuter / dogs / are / than

6 _____
a / friend / I / more / is / than / important / think / money

> **Let's build!**
> *Ask and answer using the information in Activity 1.*

> *Do you think cheetahs are more beautiful than kangaroos?*

> *No, I don't. I think kangaroos are more beautiful than cheetahs.*

2 1.12 **Read and write a–d. Then listen and check.**

Nico: What are you doing?

Emma: I'm making a hotel for insects to live in.

Nico: 1 __b__

Emma: My favourite insect is a ladybird. They're fast.

Nico: 2 ____

Emma: I like spiders, too, but they aren't insects. They've got eight eyes and eight legs.

Nico: 3 ____

Emma: Look! There's a butterfly with four colourful wings.

Nico: 4 ____

Emma: Yes. That's why I'm making an insect hotel for them.

a How amazing!

b Wow! I like insects.

c Really? I like spiders.

d That's unbelievable!

I can shine!

3 💬 **Look and read. Then talk with a partner.**

> *Guess what? Bees have got… .*

> *How amazing!*

1 Caterpillars have got twelve small eyes.

2 Butterflies can't fly when it's cold.

3 Bees have got five eyes.

4 Bees have got hair on their eyes.

Pronunciation Colour the two sounds red and blue. Crazy camels make carrot cake.

1 **Read and match. Then read and write.**

1 habitat   a To stay alive.

2 shelter   b The place in nature where an animal lives.

3 survive   c What the weather is usually like.

4 climate   d A place to sleep and be safe.

A desert is a type of ¹ ___habitat.___

Its ² _____ is hot and dry. Desert tortoises

³ _____ by eating desert plants. They

sometimes find ⁴ _____ under rocks.

2 🎧 (1.16) **Do the quiz. Listen and check. Then listen again and do the challenge.**

CRAZY CAMEL QUIZ

1 How many humps have camels got? _____

2 Where do camels live? _____

3 What do camels eat? _____

CHALLENGE!

4 Tick (✓) the camel's feet, mouth and eye.

 a

 b

 c

 d

 e

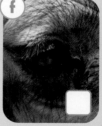 f

How can you find out more about animal habitats?

_____

8

Extra time? Think of a grassland habitat. What animals live there?

1 **Read and answer.**

1 What habitat do bald eagles live in? _____

2 Which is faster: a bald eagle or a cheetah? _____

A Description

Bald eagles are very big birds. They are brown and they've got a white head and tail.

Bald eagle

C Diet

Bald eagles eat a lot of fish. They also eat small animals, like rabbits.

B Habitat

Bald eagles live in habitats near rivers or the ocean. They find shelter in tall trees in forests.

D Comparison

Bald eagles are faster than cheetahs! Cheetahs can run fast, but bald eagles can fly faster.

2 Give it a go **Plan your fact file for an animal from your country.**

Description: Think of three describing words.	
Habitat: Where does it live?	
Diet: What does it eat?	
Comparison: How is it different to another animal?	

I can shine!

3 **Now write your fact file. Use your notes from Activity 2.**

Description: _____ are _____ .

Habitat: They live _____ .

Diet: They eat _____ .

Comparison: They're _____ .

Check your work! Check your comparisons. Remember! (fast)er / more (dangerous) than... .

9

1 **Read and complete the crossword.**

Across ➡

2 This animal is similar to a dog.
It lives in the mountains.

6 This animal is dangerous. It lives in rivers.

7 This animal is a big bird. It can fly high.

Down ⬇

1 This animal is slow. It lives in
grasslands or in the desert.

3 This animal can run very fast.
It's yellow with spots.

4 This is a small insect. It's sometimes
black and shiny.

5 This animal is white. It lives in the Arctic.

6 This animal is big. It lives in the desert.

Crossword (1 Down): t o r t o i s e

2 (1.19) **Look and write. Then listen and check.**

1 young / wolf — The cheetah is younger than the wolf.

2 slow — _____

3 dangerous — _____

4 colourful — _____

3 **Read and write. Then change the words in blue and act out.**

1 I've done my homework, *Dad.*
Really ? *(lyeral)* Well done!

2 I can stand on one leg for *ten* minutes.
That's _____! *(banluieevbel)*

3 Look over there. It's a *deer.*
_____! *(oww)*

4 My *grandmother* is *eighty* today!
How _____! *(znamiga)*

10 **Extra time?** I live in grasslands. I'm bigger than a tortoise. I jump on two legs. What am I?

1 **Think and complete. Then add another animal to each habitat. Which animal lives in all three habitats?**

~~cheetah~~ eagle tortoise wolf deer kangaroo camel beetle

grasslands	forest	desert
cheetah		

2 **Complete your journal.**

Step 1: Choose two animals.

Step 2: Write your journal.

Step 3: Find or draw pictures to decorate it.

Camels VS Desert tortoises

The same

- Camels and desert tortoises live in desert habitats.
- Camels and desert tortoises eat plants.

Different

- Camels are more dangerous than desert tortoises.
- Camels have got bigger feet than tortoises.

I like camels and desert tortoises, but my favourite animal is the camel!

The camel

3 **Think and write.**

Unit 1

An amazing animal: _____

A difficult word: _____

An interesting fact: _____

Tip!
Keep a dictionary of difficult words.

Home-school link 🔗 Tell your family about your favourite animals.

All about technology

Let's review!

Number for you.

1 ☹ 2 ☺ 3 ☺☺ 4 ☺☺☺

watching TV ☐   playing computer games ☐

watching videos ☐   coding ☐

Lesson 1 ➡ Vocabulary

1 Look and write.

① ② ③ ④ ⑤

⑥ ⑦ ⑧ ⑨ ⑩

1 l aptop   6 m_____

2 pr_____   7 c_____

3 sc_____   8 g_____

4 sp_____   9 sm_____

5 he_____   10 e-r_____

Tell me!

Which technology items can you use to read or write a story? _____

2 Look at Activity 1 and write.

1 Leo likes playing computer games. He's got a _games console._

2 Bella likes talking to her friends. She's got _____.

3 Alex likes being on time. He's _____.

4 Nadia likes photography. _____ and a laptop.

5 Sam likes listening to music. _____ and

_____.

12

Extra time? Which technology items have got screens? Compare with a partner.

1   **Listen and tick (✓). Then write the words in orange.**

How often does Annie use... ?	never	sometimes	often	usually	always
a smart watch					✓
a mobile phone					
a laptop					
a printer					
speakers					

At school, Annie ¹_____always_____ uses a smart watch, but she ²_____ uses
a mobile phone. She ³_____ uses a laptop when she goes to the ICT room.
The students ⁴_____ use printers and they ⁵_____ use speakers.

2 **Look and write.**

1 Jack _never uses a games console._____ (never)

2 Karen _____. (usually)

3 David _____. (often)

4 Naya _____. (sometimes)

5 Max and Nur _____. (always)

6 Lucas and Emma _____. (never)

I can shine! ✳

3 **Write true sentences about you and technology.**

1 _____ (always)

2 _____ (usually)

3 _____ (often)

4 _____ (sometimes)

5 _____ (never)

Extra time? Write the ten technology words in alphabetical order.

1 **Read and circle *a* or *b*.**

1 Who do Eva and Matt often visit?   a   a builder   **ⓑ** Mrs Simms

2 What animal is missing?   a   a cat   b   a dog

3 Who has got a camera?   a   Eva   b   Mrs Simms

4 Who has got a mobile phone?   a   Eva   b   Matt

5 Where's the builder?   a   in a café   b   in a van

6 Where's Mini?   a   in a café   b   in a van

2 **Read and match.**

1 Matt takes a   a   his laptop.

2 He turns on   b   the comments.

3 He uploads   c   photo.

4 He posts an   d   advertisement.

5 He reads   e   off his laptop.

6 He turns   f   the photo.

> **Let's imagine!**
> *Tell me about the story!*
>
> The story setting is _____.
> My favourite character is _____.

I can shine!

3 **How can you help people in your family with technology?**

I can help my _____ with _____.

I can _____.

I can _____.

Extra time? How does Mrs Simms help Eva in the story?

1 **Read and write.**

1 Danny always __plays football__ after school. (play football)

Today he's _____. (basketball)

2 Tara sometimes _____. (go to the park)

Today she _____. (cinema)

3 Zack often _____. (read an e-reader)

Today _____. (book)

4 Kay usually _____. (visit her friend)

Today _____. (grandma)

Let's build!

Ask and answer using the information in Activity 1.

What do you usually do after school?

I usually... .

What are you doing now?

Now I'm... .

2 (2.13) **Read and write a–d. Then listen and check.**

Megan: Look. This website asks for a photo of me.

Mark: 1 __b__

Megan: Yes, I know. And it asks me to write my address.

Mark: 2 _____

Megan: I know. Should I tell our teacher about this website?

Mark: 3 _____

Megan: OK.

Mark: 4 _____

a Yes. You should tell Mrs Baker.

b Oh dear. You shouldn't put photos of yourself online.

c And you should ask her for a good website.

d You shouldn't write your address. It isn't safe.

I can shine!

You should / shouldn't... .

3 💬 **Look and read. Then talk with a partner.**

1 I play computer games all night. I'm tired.

2 I use my laptop all day. My eyes hurt.

3 I always play in the park after school. I'm cold.

4 My friend lives in a different city. I'm sad.

Pronunciation Colour the two sounds red and blue. You cook good food from this book!

1 **Read and match. Then look and write.**

1 search the internet   **a** To talk to and see friends or family online.

2 make video calls   **b** To look for information online.

3 chat online   **c** To read letters online.

4 open emails   **d** To talk, or write short messages, to people online.

open emails	_____	_____	_____

2 🎧 2.17 **Listen and answer. Then listen again and write. *True* or *False*?**

Which phrase (1–4) from Activity 1 is *not* mentioned? _____

1 All websites are good for young people. _____False_____

2 You should ask your teacher and parents to help you find good websites. _____

3 You should open emails from people you don't know. _____

4 You shouldn't tell your parents about emails from people you don't know. _____

5 You should never chat online to people you don't know. _____

> *Write four more things you should or shouldn't do to use technology safely.*
>
> 1 _____
>
> 2 _____
>
> 3 _____
>
> 4 _____

Extra time? What technology rules are there in your school?

1 Read and answer.

1 When does Alex watch TV? _____

2 What does he do on Sunday evening? _____

BLOG *My Digital Weekend* `SEARCH`

Saturday
In the morning, I usually watch TV. At lunchtime, I always eat with my family and we never look at screens. After lunch, I often play outside. In the evening, I sometimes watch TV and talk to my family.

Sunday
In the morning, I usually do my homework. After lunch, I usually play on my games console and I sometimes chat online with my friends. In the evening, I always use my e-reader.

2 Give it a go Plan your digital weekend blog post.

What technology do you use?	always	usually	often	sometimes	never
Saturday					
Sunday					

I can shine!

3 Now write your blog post. Use your notes from Activity 2.

BLOG *My Digital Weekend* `SEARCH`

Saturday: In the morning, I _____ .

_____

_____

Sunday: _____

_____

_____

Check your work! Check your sentences. Remember! We use 'and' to connect two ideas.

1 **What can you do? Read and circle the odd one out.**

1 Play games on: a laptop / a games console / (headphones)

2 Read stories on: a games console / an e-reader / a laptop

3 Take a photo with: a camera / a printer / a mobile phone

4 Save photos on: an e-reader / a mobile phone / a laptop

5 Turn off: a speaker / an email / a screen

2 (2.20) **Order and write. Then listen and check.**

1 Sam _always plays on his games console._
plays / Sam / his / games / console / always / on

2 _____
my / on / I'm / reading / e-reader / book / a

3 _____
school / at / We / printer / a / use / sometimes

4 _____
upload / laptop / photos / onto / often / I / my

5 _____
they / Today / smart / watches / wearing / are

6 _____
her / off / mobile / phone / Carla / turns / never

3 **Complete with *You should* or *You shouldn't*. Then give more advice.**

I want to learn more English. What should I do?

1 _You should_ watch films in English.

2 _____ speak your own language in English class.

3 _____ look up every word in a dictionary.

4 _____ read books in English.

Extra time? It plays music. It hasn't got a screen. You can't wear it. What is it?

1 **Where do you usually do these activities? Think and complete.**

> ~~play on a games console~~   turn on a laptop   use a mobile phone
> use a printer   listen with headphones   wear a smart watch   read on an e-reader
> upload photos   take a photo with a camera

At school	At home	Outside
	play on a games console	

2 **Complete your journal.**

Step 1: Choose your favourite technology.

Step 2: Write your journal.

Step 3: Find or draw pictures to decorate it.

My favourite technology

 My e-reader

What is it?
It's an electronic book.

Where and how often do I use it?
I usually use my e-reader on the bus.
I always use it before I go to bed.
I sometimes use it at the weekend.

Why is it great?
My e-reader is small.
Today I'm carrying it in my school bag.
You can turn on a light and read at night.

How to stay safe?
You should only choose books for your age.

3 **Think and write.**

Unit 2

Technology I always use: _____

Technology I never use: _____

A difficult word: _____

An important safety rule: _____

Tip!
Tell your partner your safety rule and help each other stay safe.

Home-school link Tell your family about your favourite technology.

Review 1 Our lives

 1 2.22 **Listen and write.** *True* or *False*?
Then correct the false sentences.

1 Mike is reading a blog on his mobile phone. __False__

2 Clara is making a video call. _____

3 Mike lives in Australia. _____

4 He never sees kangaroos in his garden. _____

5 He usually sees eagles in his garden. _____

6 He sometimes sees crocodiles in his garden. _____

<u>1 Mike is reading a blog on his laptop.</u>

_____

_____

2 **Complete the table for you. Then ask and answer.**

How often do you see these animals?	kangaroos	eagles	crocodiles	camels	beetles
Mike	often	usually	sometimes	never	always
Me					

How often does Mike see kangaroos?

He often sees kangaroos.

 3 **Write and match. Then talk with a partner.**

1 There's a kangaroo in the garden.

2 You s_____d be careful

3 You s_____t make

a video calls with people you don't know.

b Wow! How a_____g!

c near dangerous animals.

4 Read and circle.

1 Mike's favourite animal is the
   (kangaroo) / crocodile.

2 Mike thinks kangaroos are
   more friendly / cuter than crocodiles.

3 You **should / shouldn't** touch wild
   animals.

4 Mike often takes photos with his
   mobile phone / camera.

5 Photos look **better / worse** on a
   big screen.

6 Clara can post Mike's **email /
   photos** on her blog.

To: Clara   From: Mike
Subject: **Wildlife where I live**

Hi Clara,

My favourite Australian animal is the
kangaroo. I think a kangaroo is more friendly
than a crocodile. But you shouldn't touch wild
animals. They can be dangerous.

Here are photos of a kangaroo and a crocodile.
I often take photos with my camera.

You should upload my photos onto your
laptop, not your mobile phone. The photos
look better on a big screen. You can post my
photos on your wildlife blog.

Speak soon,
Mike

Mini-project

5 Think about the questions. Write your email.

1 What's your favourite animal?
2 How is it different to another animal?
3 Which technology do you use to take photos?
4 What can people do with your photos?

To: _____   From: _____

Subject: **Wildlife where I live**

Hi _____,

_____

_____

_____

_____

_____

_____

Speak soon,

_____

Time to shine!

6 Read and tick (✓).

I can write facts about an animal.

Wow! ☐

Good! ☐

Getting better! ☐

I can compare different animals.

Wow! ☐

Good! ☐

Getting better! ☐

I can write a blog about technology.

Wow! ☐

Good! ☐

Getting better! ☐

I can talk about what happens normally and what is happening now.

Wow! ☐

Good! ☐

Getting better! ☐

3 Sharing our skills

Let's review!

Choose and write three skills you've got.

I can _____ , _____ and _____ .

1 Look and write.

1 ___rope___   6 _____
2 _____   7 _____
3 _____   8 _____
4 _____   9 _____
5 _____   10 _____

2 Look at Activity 1 and write.

1 You should wear a ___helmet___ when you ride a bike.

2 He uses a _____ to open the door.

3 She turns on her _____ to see at night.

4 I can buy a present with some of my _____ .

5 You should eat an apple for a healthy _____ .

6 I write what I do every day in my _____ .

Tell me!

What's more interesting: reading a magazine, doing a puzzle or writing a diary?

I think _____ .

Extra time? Which of the items have you got in your bedroom? Tell a partner.

1 (3.04) **Listen and answer. Then listen again and tick (✓) or cross (✗) for Nina.**

What is the one item Tim and Nina's dad hasn't got? _____

2 **Look at Activity 1 and write.**

1 Tim _doesn't have to bring a bandage._

2 He _____ .

3 He _____ .

4 Nina _____ .

5 She _____ .

6 She _____ .

I can shine! ✳

3 **Imagine you are going camping with your family. Write.**

1 I have to bring _____ .

2 I _____ .

3 I _____ .

4 I don't have to _____ .

5 I _____ .

Extra time? Choose three of the new words from Lesson 1. Draw and label them.

1 **Read and number.**

☐ Helen and Bill live in the mountains, near a family of wolves.

[1] Helen is born in New Zealand.

☐ Helen and Bill go to the desert on camels.

☐ Helen travels to the North Pole.

☐ Helen climbs her first mountain in New Zealand.

☐ Helen starts her organisation, *Adventure Classroom*.

Helen Thayer
Explorer

2 **Read and write.**

1 Helen cooks food on a <u>stove.</u> (vetso)

2 She wears _____ to keep her hands warm. (ovegsl)

3 She wears a _____ to keep her body warm. (tjkcea)

4 She travels around the North Pole on a _____ . (ldseeg)

5 She sleeps in a _____ . (isngeelp / gba)

6 Helen and Bill learn how to build a shelter with _____ . (tskaenlb)

Let's imagine!
Tell me about the story!

Helen Thayer visits _____ .

Helen is _____ .

I can shine! ✳

3 **Think of someone you know. What skills has he / she got?**

He / She can _____ .

He / She _____ .

_____

_____

Extra time? Who helps you learn new skills? Write a list.

1 Complete the questions and answers.

1 _Does_____ she _have to_____ wear a jacket at school?

No, _she doesn't._

2 _____ he _____ wear a helmet on his bike?

Yes, _____.

3 _____ we _____ go to school by bus?

Yes, _____.

4 _____ they _____ go to the park by car?

No, _____.

5 _____ he _____ bring a snack to school?

No, _____.

6 _____ she _____ take a sleeping bag?

Yes, _____.

Let's build!
Ask and answer using the information in Activity 1.

Do you have to wear a jacket at school?

Yes, I do.

2 〔3.12〕 Read and number.
Then listen and check.

☐ **Pat:** Shall we look at an online dictionary and find the answer?

☐ **Sophie:** Yes, that's a good idea, Pat.

☐ **Sophie:** Oh, thank you! That's very kind.

☐ **Sophie:** I'm doing a puzzle in my magazine, but I can't think of the correct word.

〔1〕 **Pat:** Hi, Sophie. Why are you sad?

☐ **Pat:** Oh, dear. Shall I help you?

I can shine!

3 💬 Look and read. Then talk with a partner.

1 I have to do my homework, but it's difficult.

2 I want to read my book, but I can't find it.

3 I have to wear my helmet, but I can't find it.

4 I want to finish this puzzle, but it's difficult.

I have to do my homework, but it's difficult.

Shall I help you?

Pronunciation Colour the two sounds red and blue. Clean, crazy, clever crocodiles climb.

1 **Read and match. Then look and write.**

1 float   a This is all around us, but we can't see it.

2 sink   b To stay on the top of water.

3 flat   c To go down under the water.

4 air   d To describe a surface that doesn't go up and down.

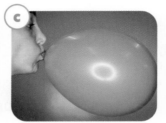

_____ *flat* _____   _____   _____   _____

2 🎧 (3.16) **What does Eva need to make the boat? Listen and tick (✓).**

① balloon   ② wood   ③ straw   ④ bottle ✓   ⑤ ball   ⑥ drum

3 🎧 (3.17) **Listen again. Then write.**

1 A plastic bottle _____, so it's good for a boat.

2 You don't want a boat that _____.

3 The _____ in the balloon makes the boat move.

How do we share our skills? Look and tick (✓).

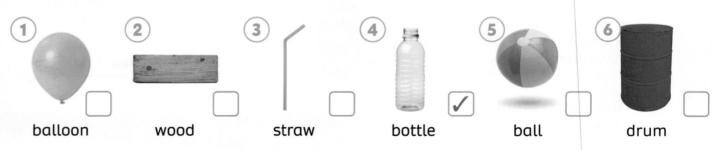

Extra time? What other things can you make with a plastic bottle?

1 **Read and answer.**

1 What do you need to make a balloon boat? _____

2 What makes the balloon boat move? _____

How to make a balloon boat

Step 1: First, cut the side of a plastic bottle, and make a hole in the bottom. Ask an adult to help you.

Step 2: Then, tie the balloon onto a plastic straw. Put the straw through the hole in the bottle.

Step 3: Finally, blow air through the straw. Put the boat in water. The air in the balloon makes your boat move.

2 Give it a go **Plan your instructions for how to make a boat.**

Tick (✓) the materials you need	a plastic bottle ☐ a box ☐ paper ☐ a plastic straw ☐
Words to use	_____ _____

I can shine!

3 **Now write your instructions and draw. Use your notes from Activity 2.**

How to make a boat

Step 1: _____

_____

_____

Step 2: _____

_____

_____

Step 3: _____

_____

_____

Check your work! Check your instructions. Remember! 1 First... 2 Then... 3 Finally...

1 **Read the riddles and write.**

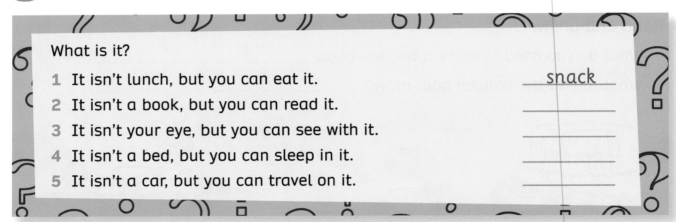

What is it?

1 It isn't lunch, but you can eat it. _____snack_____

2 It isn't a book, but you can read it. _____

3 It isn't your eye, but you can see with it. _____

4 It isn't a bed, but you can sleep in it. _____

5 It isn't a car, but you can travel on it. _____

2 (3.20) **Listen and number. Then listen again and write.**

1 Do Steve and Lucy have to wear hats? __No,__ they __don't.__

2 Do they have to wear jackets? _____ , they _____ .

3 Does Anna have to see the teacher? _____ , she _____ .

4 Does she have to ask for a bandage? _____ , she _____ .

5 Does Aunt Sue have to eat her snack now? _____ , she _____ .

6 Do Rachel and Bob have to finish a puzzle? _____ , they _____ .

3 💬 **Order and write. Then change the words in blue and act out.**

Katy: Are you OK?

Zak: No, I'm not. I can't find my diary.

Katy: _____ ? I / Shall / you / help

Zak: Thank you. _____ That's / kind / very

Katy: Let's look under the bed.

Zak: That's a good idea.

Extra time? Write a riddle for 'key': It isn't... , but it... . What is it?

1 **Where do you usually use the objects? Think and complete.**

> ~~diary~~ jacket rope puzzle magazine sledge
> blanket gloves torch sleeping bag money helmet

Inside

diary _____ _____

_____ _____

_____ _____

Outside

_____ _____

_____ _____

2 **Complete your journal.**

Step 1: Choose where to go on a three-day school trip.

Step 2: Write your journal.

Step 3: Find or draw pictures to decorate it.

Cabins in the forest

Packing my bag!

- I have to take a sleeping bag.
  It's cold inside at night.
- I have to take a torch.
  We go outside at night.
- I don't have to take magazines.
  There are a lot of books inside the cabin.

Sharing skills!

- I can teach my friends how to make a den.
- I want to learn how to make a fire.

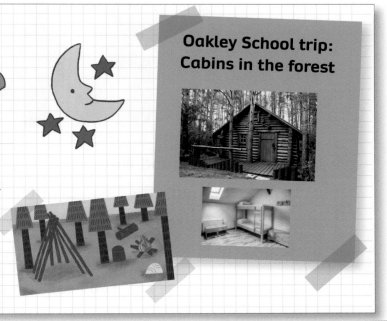

Oakley School trip:
Cabins in the forest

3 **Think and write.**

Unit 3

My favourite object: _____

A difficult word: _____

A new skill: _____

Tip!
Get organised.
Make a list of things
you have to take
to school.

Home-school link 📥 Tell your family about your school trip.

4 Let's celebrate

Lesson 1 ➡ Vocabulary

1 Look and write.

1 b<u>and</u>_____
2 d_____
3 f_____
4 p_____
5 m_____
6 c_____
7 f_____
8 L_____
9 b_____
10 c_____

2 Look at Activity 1 and write.

1 In photo a <u>there are</u> four <u>drums.</u>

2 In photo b <u>there are</u> colourful _____.

3 In photo c _____ a _____ in the street.

4 In photo d _____ two people wearing _____ and _____.

5 In photo e _____ white _____ and colourful _____.

6 In photo f _____ seven _____ on the cake.

Tell me!

What things do you usually have at a birthday party?

_____

Extra time? Write the ten celebration words in alphabetical order.

1 Listen and tick (✓) or cross (✗). Then write.

1 _____There was_____ a big birthday cake.

2 _____ a small birthday cake.

3 _____ fifty candles on the cake.

4 _____ any costumes or masks.

5 _____ a band in the house.

6 _____ a band in the garden.

2 Look and write about Tom's party.

1 There weren't __any fireworks.__

2 There was _____ .

3 _____

4 _____

5 _____

6 _____

I can shine!

3 Write about a birthday party last year.

1 There was _____ .

2 _____

3 There wasn't _____ .

4 _____

Extra time? Look at Photo d in Lesson 1. Cover, remember and write.

1 **Read and circle.**

There was a ¹(village) / city in China. It was New Year and there was a scary ²**dragon** / **lion** called Nian. There was a ³**dangerous** / **brave** man in the village. That night, there were ⁴**songs** / **fireworks** and noisy drums. The next day, there ⁵**was** / **wasn't** a dragon in the village. Today in China, there's a ⁶**festival** / **cake** to celebrate New Year.

2 **Remember the story. Cross (✗) the word that isn't correct.**

The dragon was… .		hungry ☐	surprised ☐	thirsty ☐
The people were… .		surprised ☐	frightened ☐	hungry ☐
The old man was… .		frightened ☐	tired ☐	dirty ☐

Let's imagine!

Tell me about the story!

The story setting is _____.

My favourite character is _____.

I can shine!

3 **Think about New Year in your country. Write.**

1 When do you celebrate New Year?

_____

2 How do you celebrate New Year?

_____

_____

Extra time? Remember the story. What three things was the dragon frightened of?

1 **Write the questions. Then match.**

1 <u>Where was your mum yesterday?</u> Where / your mum / yesterday [c]

2 _____? Who / at / the parade [ ]

3 _____? he / frightened [ ]

4 _____? Where / your friends / yesterday [ ]

5 _____? When / the party [ ]

6 _____? your friends / happy [ ]

a No, he wasn't. d They were at a party.

b It was in the evening. e Dan and Nina were there.

c She was at the bank. f Yes, they were.

Let's build!
Ask and answer the questions in Activity 1.

Where was your mum yesterday?

She was... .

2  **Read and write a–d. Then listen and check.**

Leila: 1 _C_

Jack: It's a kransekage.

Leila: 2 _____

Jack: Kransekage.

Leila: 3 _____

Jack: It's a tall cake from Denmark. We eat it at New Year. Do you understand?

Leila: 4 _____

Jack: It's k-r-a-n-s-e-k-a-g-e.

a Can you say that again, please?

b Yes, thanks. How do you spell kransekage?

c What are you eating? It looks delicious!

d What does kransekage mean?

I can shine!

3 **Look and read. Then ask and answer.**

What's this?

Can you say that again, please?

1 sari
(from India)

What does it mean?

How do you spell it?

2 poncho
(from Peru)

Pronunciation Colour the two sounds red and blue. Please repeat your idea in my ear.

33

1 **Read and match. Then look and write.**

1 sky
2 stars
3 sun
4 moon

a They're balls of gas and we see them in the sky at night.
b It's above us and it's often blue in the day.
c It travels around Earth and we see it in the sky at night.
d It's a big star and it gives us light and heat in the day.

_____moon_____ _____ _____ _____

2 🎧 4.16 **Listen and tick (✓). Then listen again and write.**

Country: Malta_____
Month: _____
Festival: _____
Celebrates: _____
_____
Was it good? _____

Why do you think people all over the world like festivals?
Festivals are _____ and _____ for everybody.

Extra time? What things do you do at your favourite festival?

1 **Read and answer.**

1 Was Molly's opinion of the Carnival positive or negative? _____

2 What words does she use to describe the carnival? _____

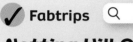 Fabtrips 🔍 _____

Notting Hill Carnival

Last weekend, I was at the Notting Hill Carnival, in London. There was a parade with children in beautiful costumes and colourful masks. There were amazing bands with drums from the Caribbean. There were a lot of people at the carnival and the streets were dirty. But there was delicious food from lots of different countries.
It was great fun. You should go!

2 **Give it a go** **Plan your review of a special event.**

Event		Clothes	
When?		Music	
Where?		Food	

I can shine!

3 **Now write your review. Use your notes from Activity 2.**

✔ Fabtrips 🔍 _____   **sign in**

_____

_____

_____

_____

_____

_____

Check your work! Improve your review. Add two more words to describe the event.

35

1 **Read and write. Then order the letters in blue to find the missing word.**

1 These colourful objects have got air inside them. b a l l o o n s

2 I want to drink water. I'm… . ___ ___ ___ ◯ ___ ___ ___

3 This is a group of people who play music together. ___ ◯ ___ ___

4 I need to wash my hands. They're… . ◯ ___ ___ ___

5 These types of lights don't use electricity. ___ ___ ___ ___ ◯ ___

6 Oh, wow! A party! I'm… . ___ ___ ___ ◯ ___ ___ ___ ___

7 People wear costumes, go along a street and play music.

Missing word: ___ ___ ___ ___ ___ ___

2 **Write the questions. Then listen and answer.**

1 Where / Danny / at the weekend Where was Danny at the weekend?
   He was at a street party.

2 When / the party _____ ?

_____

3 Who / at the party _____ ?

_____

4 Were / Danny's friends / hungry _____ ?

_____

5 Were / balloons? _____ ?

_____

6 Was / band? _____ ?

_____

3 **Order and write. Then choose a new word and play.**

Omar: Let's play a dictionary game. My word is 'ashiko'.

Zoe: 1 _____ ? does / What / mean / it

Omar: It's a drum from West Africa.

Zoe: 2 _____ ? you / How / it / do / spell

Omar: It's a-s-h-i-k-o.

My word: _____   My partner's word: _____

Extra time? What am I? Look and order. k f i w r o e s r

1 Think about your favourite festival last year. Complete.

> parade   balloons   dirty   thirsty   flags   candles   band   frightened
> fireworks   tired   drums   hungry   costumes   masks   surprised   lights

There was… .	There were… .	I was… .

There wasn't… .	There weren't any… .	I wasn't… .

2 Complete your journal.

Step 1: Choose your favourite festival from last year.

Step 2: Write your journal.

Step 3: Find or draw pictures to decorate it.

Summer School Fair

Where was it?
It was in the school playground.

Activities:
There were races and games.
There were candles and masks to buy.

Music:
There was an amazing band.

Clothes:
There weren't any costumes.

Food:
There were burgers and there was ice cream.

Were you happy?
Yes, but I was hot and tired!

3 Think and write.

Unit 4

My favourite festival word: _____

A difficult word: _____

My favourite celebration from another country:

_____

Tip!
Use the internet and books to find out more about international celebrations.

Home-school link Tell your family about your favourite festival from last year.

37

Review 2 Our world

International Festival

1 🎧 4.21 **Listen and circle. Then listen again and check.**

1 Olivia **was** / **wasn't** at the International Festival last year.

2 There were traditional costumes with **red** / **blue** jackets and brown **hats** / **helmets**.

3 There was a **sledge** / **sleeping bag** at the Canadian stall.

4 In Canada you **have to** / **don't have to** travel by sledge in the snow.

5 There's a red maple leaf on the **poster** / **costume**.

6 Josh wants to buy some Canadian **masks** / **snacks**.

2 💬 **Look and write. Then ask and answer.**

Things you have to take to the International Festival.

a snack	a mask	gloves	money	a costume	a diary
✗	✗	✓	✓	✗	✓

I have to take _____gloves_____, _____ and _____.

I don't _____.

< _Do you have to take... ?_ | _Yes, I do. / No, I don't._ >

3 💬 **Write and match. Then talk with a partner.**

1 What does maple m_____?   a Thank you. That's very kind.

2 How do you s_____ it?   b It's a Canadian tree.

3 Shall I h_____ you?   c It's m–a–p–l–e.

4 Read and write.

1 What country does this poster represent?

India

2 What's lassi?

_____

3 What can you listen to?

_____

4 What can you buy?

_____

5 What do you use to open the boxes?

_____

6 What do you have to bring?

_____

Welcome to the International Festival

Visit the India stall

Are you thirsty? Try our traditional Indian drink, lassi. It's a delicious yoghurt and fruit drink.

Are you hungry? Try our beautiful Indian snacks.

Come and listen to the traditional Indian band.

Do you want to buy some presents?

There are lots of colourful candles. There are special boxes you can open with keys.

Remember, you have to bring some money.

Mini-project

5 Imagine you were at the International Festival. Write your diary entry.

Last Sunday

Last Sunday, I was at _____

_____.

There was a stall from _____

_____.

At the stall, _____

_____

_____.

I was _____

_____

_____.

Time to shine!

6 Read and tick (✓).

I can write instructions for an outdoor activity.

Wow! ☐

Good! ☐

Getting better! ☐

I can write a review about a festival in the past.

Wow! ☐

Good! ☐

Getting better! ☐

I can ask and answer about what people have to / don't have to do.

Wow! ☐

Good! ☐

Getting better! ☐

I can ask and answer about the past using *there was / wasn't* and *there were / weren't*.

Wow! ☐

Good! ☐

Getting better! ☐

5 Being kind

Let's review!

Write.

play _____   visit _____

go to _____   watch _____

1 Look and write.

1 _offer_ someone your seat

2 _____ food

3 _____ a fence

4 _____ the windows

5 _____ a dog

6 _____ the rubbish

7 _____ the plants

8 _____ a child

9 _____ someone

10 _____ shopping

2 Look at photos 1–6 in Activity 1 and write.

1 The man _is offering someone his seat._

2 She _____.

3 She _____.

4 _____.

5 _____.

6 _____.

Tell me!
Which activities do you do every week?

I _____.

Extra time? Which activities do you do inside and outside?

1 **Listen and number. Then write.**

a b c 1 d e

1 First, Andy _cleaned the windows_ in their car.

2 Then, he _____ .

3 After lunch, _____ .

4 Then, _____ .

5 Finally, _____ .

2 **Look and write about last Saturday.**

1 2 3 4 5 6

1 Laura _didn't visit her friends._

2 She _____ .

3 _____ .

4 Tariq _____ .

5 He _____ .

6 _____ .

I can shine! ✳

3 **Write for you.**

Last Saturday, I _____ .

I didn't _____ .

Extra time? Write the headings *help*, *share*, *tidy* and *visit*. What words go with them?

1 **Read and match.**

1 What does Ravi want?   **a** a blanket

2 What does his mum give him?   **b** a drum

3 What does the woman give Ravi? **c** some wood

4 What does the father give Ravi? **d** a drum

5 What does the man give Ravi?   **e** some bread

6 What does the musician give Ravi? **f** a horse

> **Let's imagine!**
> *Tell me about the story!*
>
> *The story setting is* _____ .
>
> *My favourite character is* _____ .

2 **Read and write.**

| cry   try   smile   laugh   arrive   ~~pick up~~ |

1 Ravi's mum __picked up__ some wood for him.

2 A woman _____ because Ravi gave her wood for her fire.

3 A girl _____ because she was hungry.

4 Ravi _____ home with his drum.

5 Ravi's mum _____ and clapped her hands.

6 Ravi got his drum because he _____ to help everyone.

I can shine!

3 **How are you kind to others? Write.**

I'm kind because I _____

_____ .

Yesterday, I _____

_____ .

Extra time? Think about your favourite scene in the story. Why do you like it?

1 **Write the questions. Then look and write the answers.**

1 Al / go / to school / yesterday

<u>Did Al go to school yesterday?</u> ✓ <u>Yes, he did.</u>

2 Lisa / look after / her brother / on Sunday

_____ ? ✗ _____

3 Jake and Tina / paint a fence / last week

_____ ? ✓ _____

4 Where / Luis / walk the dog

_____ ?

_____ (park)

5 When / Kate / arrive home

_____ ?

_____ (six o'clock)

6 What / Jo and Tom / do / on Saturday

_____ ?

_____ (water / plants)

Let's build!
Ask and answer using the information in Activity 1.

Did you go to school yesterday?

No, I didn't.

2 🎧 5.12 **Read and number. Then listen and check.**

☐ **Rosa:** I'm dirty because I helped Grandad today.

☐ **Rosa:** He was tired so I walked his dog. Can I have a snack, please? I'm hungry.

1 **Mum:** Oh Rosa! Why are you dirty?

☐ **Mum:** It's only three o'clock. Why are you hungry?

☐ **Rosa:** I'm hungry because I shared my lunch with Grandad!

☐ **Mum:** That was kind of you. Why did he need help?

I can shine! ✳

3 💬 **Read and think. Then ask and answer.**

Why are you dirty?

Why are you hungry?

Why are you thirsty?

Why are you tired?

Pronunciation Colour the two sounds red and blue.
Luca looked and waited. He worked and painted.

1 **Read and match. Then read and write.**

1 project
2 donate
3 collect money
4 volunteer

a To get money from different people.
b To give something.
c To offer your help for nothing.
d A planned activity.

At school, we ¹ <u>collect money</u> from everyone for new laptops. My parents also ² _____ £3 every year to help the local library. In my village, our community ³ _____ is to plant trees in the park. I also ⁴ _____ to tidy up rubbish on the beach every week.

2 🎧 5.16 **Listen and tick (✓). Then listen again and circle.**

a

b

My **school** / **family** collected money for a community project. Families donated **old** / **new** books. We invited people into the **school** / **park**. My **class** / **teacher** volunteered to sell children's books. We collected money for **flowers** / **trees**. We planted them in the **park** / **school playground**.

How can schools help people in the community?

Schools can _____.

Extra time? Who do you help in your community? Tell a partner.

1 **Read and answer.**

1 Why did Diana want to collect money? _____

2 How did she finish the race? _____

My egg and spoon race, by Diana

Last weekend, there was a race at school. We wanted to collect money for a community project. People donated money if we finished the race with an egg on a spoon. We started running. Then, I looked down and my egg wasn't on the spoon. So, I picked up a stone and finished the race with the stone on my spoon.

In the end, everyone clapped and laughed when I arrived. We collected a lot of money!

2 **Give it a go** **Plan your story about a past sports event.**

What event?	
When?	
Where?	
What happened… at the start? in the middle? in the end?	

I can shine!

3 **Now write your story. Use your notes from Activity 2.**

_____

_____

_____

_____

_____

_____

Check your work! Check you've included a clear start, middle and end.

1 **Order and write.**

1 the / plants / water <u>water the plants</u>

2 carry / shopping / the _____

3 your / look / brother / after / little _____

4 Dad's / laugh / jokes / at _____

5 rubbish / up / your / tidy _____

6 food / your / with / share / sister _____

7 fence / paint / a _____

8 your / Grandma / to / offer / seat _____

2 (5.19) **Read and write. Then listen and check.**

| help | ~~smile~~ | arrive | not clean | ~~visit~~ | cry | pick up |

Last week…

1 He ___<u>smiled</u>___ at a girl who was sad.

2 They _____ the windows in their bedrooms.

3 We _____ shells on the beach.

4 ___<u>Did she visit</u>___ her cousin in hospital? No, she didn't.

5 _____ at the sad film? Yes, I did.

6 _____ their brother with his homework? No, they didn't.

7 When _____ she _____ home yesterday? At five o'clock.

3 💬 **Look and write. Then change the words in blue and act out.**

I'm tired because I walked the dog.   I'm tired!   Why are you tired?

1 _____

2 _____

3 _____

Extra time? Think of four actions you can do with food.

What I did last week

What I did yesterday

1 Think and complete.

share	paint
water	cry
clean	pick up
laugh	offer
tidy up	arrive
carry	smile
visit	look
try	walk

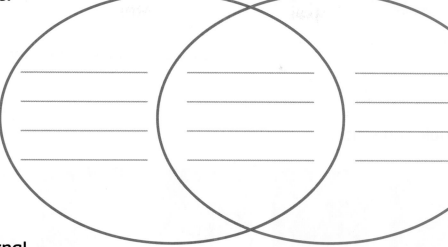

2 Complete your journal.

Step 1: Think about last week. What did you do? How were you kind?

Step 2: Write your journal.

Step 3: Find or draw pictures to decorate it.

Last week

Monday
I visited Grandma after school and we walked the dog in the park.

Tuesday
I arrived home at six o'clock, after football practice. I was tired.

Wednesday
I looked after my little brother and he didn't cry!

Thursday
I tidied up my bedroom.

Friday
I watched a film with my family and we laughed.

Saturday
I didn't visit my cousins.

Sunday
I watered the plants in the garden with my dad.

3 Think and write.

Unit 5

My favourite way to be kind: _____

A difficult word: _____

Something I can do to help someone next week:

_____

Tip!
We often write about yesterday by adding –ed to an action word.

Home-school link 🔀 Tell your family about how you were kind last week.

47

Our important places

Let'sreview!

Write three places you can visit in a city.

_____ _____ _____

1 Look and write.

1 p<u>ack</u>   a s<u>uitcase</u>

2 s_____   in a h_____

3 r_____   a g_____

4 g_____   s_____

5 t_____   by b_____

6 w_____   in a q_____

7 b_____   a t_____

8 t_____   a t_____

9 e_____   m_____

10 g_____   on a t_____

2 Look at Activity 1 and write.

Maya's holiday last year

1 (Photo 1) She <u>packed her suitcase.</u>

2 (Photo 2) Her family _____.

3 (Photo 5) They _____ to the museum.

4 (Photo 6) Her dad _____ to buy a ticket.

5 (Photo 9) Her mum _____ at the bank.

Tell me!
*What activities do you do
before you go on holiday?*

_____

Extra time? What do you do before you visit a museum? Compare with a partner.

1   **Listen and tick (✓) or cross (✗). Then write.**

Cristina	✓				
Max					

1 Cristina and Max <u>are going to pack their suitcases.</u>
2 Cristina is going to travel _____.
3 Max isn't _____.
4 Max is _____.
5 They _____.
6 They _____.

2 **Read, think and write. Use *going to*.**

| ~~stay in a hotel~~   go sightseeing   exchange money   take a taxi   buy a ticket |

1 They're carrying suitcases. <u>They're going to stay in a hotel.</u>
2 She's waiting in a queue. _____
3 He's reading a guidebook. _____
4 We want to buy things. _____
5 They're tired of walking. _____

I can shine! ✳

3 **Imagine you're going to go on holiday tomorrow. Write.**

1 ✓   I'm going to _____.
2 ✗   I'm not going to _____.
3 ✓   _____
4 ✗   _____
5 ✓   _____

Extra time? Draw and label four holiday activities.

1 Read and write a–g.

Lara's Madrid plans

<u>Sunday 4th April</u>

[b]

<u>Monday 5th April</u>

[ ] [ ]

<u>Tuesday 6th April</u>

[ ] [ ]

<u>Wednesday 7th April</u>

[ ] [ ]

a They're going to travel to Madrid.

~~b She's going to pack her suitcase.~~

c They're going to see some amazing places.

d She's going to send a postcard.

e They're going to go on a tour of the stadium.

f They're going to play football in the park.

g The Spanish team is going to meet them.

2 Read and circle a or b. Then write.

1 How are they going to travel to the airport?

a   (b)   <u>minibus</u>

2 How are they going to travel around Madrid?

a   b   _____

3 What is Lara going to travel on for the first time?

a   b   _____

4 How are they going to travel to the football stadium?

a   b   _____

Let's imagine!
Tell me about the diary!
The diary is about
_____.

My favourite day is
_____.

I can shine!

3 Plan your perfect holiday.

1 When are you going to go? _____

2 Where are you going to go? _____

3 How are you going to travel? _____

4 What are you going to do? _____

Extra time? How do you like to travel? Tell a partner.

1 **Read the answers and write the questions.**
Use *How*, *Where*, *What*, *Who* and *When*.

1 Where is she going to go?

She's going to go to the beach.

2 _____

She's going to travel by bus.

3 _____

They're going to go to a museum.

4 _____

They're going to arrive at ten o'clock.

5 _____

He's going to watch a film.

6 _____

He's going to meet his friend.

> **Let's build!**
> *Ask and answer using the information in Activity 1.*

> *Where are you going to go next Saturday?*

> *I'm going to go to the cinema.*

2 🎧 **6.12** **Read and number. Then listen and check.**

☐ I disagree. Theatre tickets are very expensive.

☐ That's a good idea. It's interesting, but it's going to be very busy.

☐ You're right. They're expensive. There's a great boat trip on the river.

☐ How about a bike tour of the city? Bike tours are great.

[1] Let's do something fun tomorrow. How about the Science Museum?

☐ Yes, great idea. Let's go on a boat trip tomorrow.

☐ I disagree. I don't like bike tours. The theatre is better.

☐ I agree. OK, so not the Science Museum.

I can shine!

> *What shall we do tomorrow?*

3 💬 **Read and think.**
Then talk with a partner.

> *How about... ?*

> *I agree! / I disagree!*

Pronunciation Colour the two sounds red and blue. **St**an **sp**eaks about **st**orms in **Sp**ain.

1 **Read and match. Then write.**

1 accommodation   a The way a group of people live (food, clothes, music).

2. souvenir   b A place where someone can live or stay.

3 ecotourism   c An object people buy to help them remember a holiday.

4 culture   d A holiday that helps the environment and local people.

accommodation   _____   _____   _____

2 🎧 6.16 **Listen and tick (✓). Then write.**

1 transport

2 accommodation

3 ecotourism activity

4 souvenir

Emma and her family are going to travel to Austria by ^{1}___ferry___ and train.

They aren't going to stay in a ^{2}_____. They're going to stay on a ^{3}_____.

They're going to help ^{4}_____ the animals. Emma's going to buy

David a ^{5}_____.

Why is ecotourism good? Write two reasons.

_____

_____

Extra time? Do you like travelling? Why? / Why not?

1 **Read and answer.**

1 What is Lisa going to do on Thursday? _____

2 How does Lisa feel about her holiday plans? _____

○ ● ○

Hi Marco,

We're having a fantastic time here in Fiji!

We travelled here by ferry. Our accommodation is great! We're staying in a traditional house in a small village. We have dinner with local families. They're teaching us about their culture.

Tomorrow, we're going to join an ecotourism project and help plant trees in the forest. On Thursday, we're going to go snorkelling in the ocean. There are colourful fish and plants to see. In the afternoon, we're going to go on a bus tour. I'm very excited about our plans.

From, Lisa

2 Give it a go **Plan your holiday email.**

Where?	
How / travel?	
Accommodation	
Ecotourism activities	
Future plans	

I can shine! ✳

3 **Now write your email. Use your notes from Activity 2.**

○ ● ○

_____

_____

_____

_____

_____

_____

Check your work! Improve your email. Check your spelling of new words in a dictionary. **53**

1 **Read and write.**

David is going to pack a ¹_____ suitcase _____ (cutsaies). Then, he's going to travel by
²_____ (udreundorng) to the ³_____ (ptiorar). Finally he's
going to ⁴_____ (eakt a xiat) to the ⁵_____ (letho).
He's going to ⁶_____ (taiw ni a eequu) because he wants to
⁷_____ (uyb a ttekic) for the ⁸_____ (bleac rca).
It's a good way to ⁹_____ (og sisgneihteg).

2 🎧 (6.19) **Write the questions and answers. Then listen and check.**

1 What's / tomorrow / going to / Karen / do / ?

What's Karen going to do tomorrow?

She's going to _____.

She isn't going to _____.

2 at the weekend / Where's / Paul / go / going to / ?

_____

_____

_____

3 going to / are / Who / tonight / they / visit / ?

_____

_____

_____

3 💬 **Read and write _I agree_ or _I disagree_. Then talk with a partner.**

1 _A beach holiday is better than a city holiday._

_____! I love the beach.

2 _Tourism is good for a city._

_____! Tourism can make a city noisier.

3 _Travelling by plane is better than by train._

_____! Planes are worse for the environment.

4 _Visiting different countries is important._

_____! It's great to see how other people live.

54

Extra time? This form of transport goes up and down, but it isn't a plane. What is it?

1 **Think and complete. Then add an extra phrase to each category.**

> ~~pack a suitcase~~ go to the airport   stay in a hotel   buy a ticket
> read a guidebook   take a taxi   wait in a queue   travel by underground

Before you go on holiday

___pack a suitcase___

_____

_____

Before you go on a tour

_____

_____

_____

Holidays

Travel

_____

_____

_____

_____

Accommodation

_____

_____

2 **Complete your journal.**

Step 1: Choose a place you want to visit. Plan your holiday there.

Step 2: Write your journal.

Step 3: Find or draw pictures to decorate it.

My perfect holiday

Paris

Where are you going to go?
I'm going to go to Paris.

How are you going to travel?
I'm going to travel by
underground in Paris.

What are you going to do?
I'm going to exchange money.
Then, I'm going to go on a boat tour.
I also want to go up the Eiffel Tower. I'm
going to buy my ticket online so I don't
have to wait in a very long queue.

3 **Think and write.**

Unit 6

An important holiday activity: _____

My favourite way to travel: _____

A difficult word: _____

Tip!
You can say
take a or _travel by_
when you talk about
transport.

Home-school link Tell your family about your perfect holiday.

Review 3 Our future

1 🎧 6.21 **Listen and circle. Then write.**

1 Did Tom pack his suitcase yesterday?

(Yes, he did.)/ No, he didn't.

2 Did Tom's mum exchange money yesterday?

Yes, she did. / No, she didn't.

3 How are they going to travel?

By ferry and coach. / By ferry and taxi.

4 Did Tom's parents stay in the hotel last year?

Yes, they did. / No, they didn't.

5 What sanctuary are they going to visit?

An animal sanctuary. / A plant sanctuary.

6 What is Tom going to do there?

Tidy up rubbish. / Walk the dogs.

a Tom _packed his suitcase yesterday._

b Tom's mum _____.

c They _____.

d Tom's parents _____.

e They _____.

f Tom _____.

2 **Ask and answer.**

Where did you stay on your last holiday?

What did you do?

Where are you going to go this year?

How are you going to get there?

3 **Write and match. Then talk with a partner.**

1 ___Why___ are you happy?

2 I think we should take a taxi.

3 I think it's good to look after animals.

a I d_____ . A taxi is expensive.

b I a_____ . They're important.

c I'm happy b_____ I'm going to go on holiday.

4 Read and answer.

1 What animal did Mr and Mrs Rigby help?

   They helped a rabbit.

2 When did the Rigby Animal Sanctuary open?

   _____

3 What are visitors going to do?

   _____

   _____

4 How can you travel to the sanctuary?

   _____

   _____

Mini-project

5 Imagine you were at the Rigby Animal Sanctuary. Write your review.

REVIEW: Volunteer day

Things I did...

I _____

_____

_____ .

Things I'm going to do next time...
I'm going to _____

_____

_____ .

How did you travel there?
I travelled _____ .

STAR RATING! ☆☆☆

Rigby Animal Sanctuary

How did it start?

One day, Mr and Mrs Rigby helped a rabbit with a bad leg in their garden. Then, they decided to start a project. They wanted to look after sick animals. Their sanctuary opened in 1990.

Volunteer day!

This weekend, they're going to have a volunteer day. Visitors are going to walk the dogs, look after the rabbits, carry food to the horses, tidy up rubbish and more.

You can travel to the sanctuary by minibus or take a taxi. Come early so you don't have to wait in a queue!

Time to shine!

6 Read and tick (✓).

I can write a story about an event.

Wow! ☐
Good! ☐
Getting better! ☐

I can write an email about my future plans.

Wow! ☐
Good! ☐
Getting better! ☐

I can ask and answer about the past.

Wow! ☐
Good! ☐
Getting better! ☐

I can ask and answer about my holiday plans.

Wow! ☐
Good! ☐
Getting better! ☐

Goodbye from the Great Places team

1 **Think and write.**

1 look after   _a tortoise_ _____

2 wear   _____   _____

3 turn on/off   _____   _____

4 read   _____   _____

5 travel by   _____   _____

> a helmet   a child
> underground
> ~~a tortoise~~   ferry
> a mask   a torch
> a magazine
> a laptop   a guidebook

2 (7.04) **Listen and number. Then listen again and write.**

a   b   c [1]

d   e   f

1 You ____have to____ take money if you want to buy a souvenir.

2 She _____ uses her mobile phone, but she isn't _____ it now.

3 A crocodile is _____ than a tortoise.

4 There was a parade and _____ beautiful fireworks.

5 Last World Kindness Day, I _____ the fence.

6 The boy is _____ to buy a ticket.

3 💬 **Order and write. Then ask and answer.**

1 <u>How often do you use a camera?</u>
   do / camera / How / you / often / use / a / ?

2 _____
   snack / to / Do / have / a / you / take / to / school?

3 _____
   yesterday / Where / were / you / ?

4 _____
   next / What / do / going / to / weekend / you / are / ?

My town: A great place to live, by Jon

In the past, Bedford was smaller than it is today. Now it's a big town. In Bedford Library you can use computers or your laptop, but you shouldn't use your mobile phone.

I often volunteer at the Community Garden Project. I usually water the plants and tidy up the rubbish. Next month, we're going to paint fences. At Woburn Safari Park, you can see animals like bears, camels and snakes.

Last year, I loved the River Festival. There were interesting bands and beautiful fireworks. You have to take money to buy snacks. You can travel to Bedford by car, train or coach and stay in a hotel.

4 **Read and answer.**

1 Was Bedford bigger or smaller in the past? __It was smaller.__

2 Which technology can you use in the library? _____

3 What's Jon going to paint next month? _____

4 What animals can you see at the Safari Park? _____

5 Why did Jon love the River Festival? _____

6 Where can you stay in Bedford? _____

5 💬 **Talk about where you live with a partner. Why is it a great place?**

Think about...	History Animals	Technology Festivals	Community projects Transport / Accommodation

I can shine!

6 **Complete your journal.**

Step 1: Think about your favourite things in *Rise and Shine.*

Step 2: Write your journal.

Step 3: Find or draw pictures to decorate it.

Goodbye to the Great Places team!

My favourite character is Bella because she likes animals.

My favourite journal page was about a school trip because I like being with my friends.

My favourite words were about festivals and they were balloons , candles and masks .

My favourite fact: It's important to look after animals. I always walk my dog after school.

Home-school link 🔗 Tell your family about the Great Places team.

59

Mother Language Day

1 Write the languages.

1 (rsukiTh) _____ 2 (bcaAri) _____ 3 (hpianSs) _____

2 🎧 8.05 💬 **Read and write a–c. Listen and check. Then ask and answer for you.**

Lily: What's Mother Language Day?

Josh: 1 _____

Lily: What's your first language?

Josh: It's English.

Lily: What other languages can you speak?

Josh: 2 _____

Lily: Wow! Can you say something in Japanese?

Josh: 3 _____

a Let me think, I can speak Spanish and some Japanese.

b Well, it's the day we celebrate our first language.

c Wait a minute! Sayonara – that's *goodbye* in Japanese.

International Day of Happiness

3 Read and write.

relatives   sunset   circus   ~~rainbow~~

1 You can see this in the sky. It got lots of colours. __rainbow__

2 You can watch this in the evening when the sun goes down. _____

3 These people are part of your family. You can visit them. _____

4 You can go to this place and laugh. _____

4 🎧 8.10 💬 **Read and number. Listen and check. Then ask and answer for you.**

☐ Ava: Me, too. I love rainbows.

☐ Ben: Well, I love going camping. What about you?

1 Ava: What's the International Day of Happiness?

☐ Ben: No, I don't like the circus, but seeing rainbows makes me happy.

☐ Ava: No, I don't like camping, but I love going to the circus. And you?

☐ Ben: It's a day when you think about what makes you happy.

☐ Ava: Oh, yes. And what makes you happy?

World Children's Day

5 Write the words.

1 (yojne) __enjoy__
2 (marde) _____
3 (ahct) _____
4 (nijo) _____
5 (dnfi uto) _____
6 (neral) _____

6 💬 Read and write a–c. Listen and check. Then act out.

Toby: Today is World Children's Day. How are you celebrating?

Vera: I want to join a reading club because I enjoy reading.

Toby: 1 _____ I like reading, too.

Vera: And I want to find out about children in other countries.

Toby: 2 _____ Today is about children everywhere.

Vera: That's why I'm chatting to children in Mexico. I'm online now.

Toby: 3 _____ Can I say hello?

a That's very exciting.
b That sounds fun.
c That's a great idea.

International Day of Friendship

7 Write. Use *a, e, i, o, u*.

1 post _a_ c_a_rd
2 b__ k__nd t__ fr____nds
3 g__v____ pr__s__nt
4 __nv__t__ fr____nds t__ __ p__rty
5 t__xt y____r fr____nds
6 m____t fr____nds __ft__r sch____l

8  💬 Read and number. Listen and check. Then ask and answer for you.

[ ] Rik: Do you think it's important to be kind to friends?

[ ] Amy: I think it's really important to be kind to everyone.

[ ] Rik: That's right! Then, we can all be friends!

[ ] Amy: Yes, I do. In my opinion, friendship is very important.

[1] Rik: Do you like the International Day of Friendship?

[ ] Amy: Well, people can give friends a present or post them a card.

[ ] Rik: Definitely! How can people celebrate it?

Word connections

 Things

Unit 2

camera   mobile phone
e-reader   printer
games console   screen
headphones   smart watch
laptop   speaker

Unit 3

bandage   money
diary   puzzle
helmet   rope
key   snack
magazine   torch

blanket   sledge
gloves   sleeping bag
jacket   stove

Unit 4

balloons   fireworks
band   flags
candles   lights
costumes   masks
drums   parade

 Shine on!

_____
_____
_____
_____
_____
_____
_____
_____
_____
_____
_____

Describing

Unit 1

dangerous	intelligent
friendly	safe
important	young

Unit 4

dirty	surprised
frightened	thirsty
hungry	tired

 Shine on!

_____

_____

_____

_____

_____

_____

_____

_____

_____

_____

Places and travel

Welcome

bridge	fields
building	flat
city centre	hills
city hall	street
farm	village
Argentina	Spain
China	Turkey
Italy	UK
Mexico	USA
Poland	

Unit 6

airport	ferry
cable car	minibus
coach	underground

 Shine on!

_____

_____

_____

_____

_____

_____

_____

_____

_____

_____

_____

Activities

Unit 2

post an advertisement
print photos
turn off

turn on
upload photos
write comments

Unit 5

carry shopping
clean the windows
look after a child
offer someone your
   seat
paint a fence

share food
tidy up the rubbish
visit someone
walk a dog
water the plants

 **Shine on!**

Unit 6

buy a ticket
exchange money
go on a tour
go sightseeing
pack a suitcase

read a guidebook
stay in a hotel
take a taxi
travel by bus
wait in a queue

 Animals

Unit 1

beetle
camel
cheetah
crocodile
deer

eagle
kangaroo
polar bear
tortoise
wolf

 Shine on!